Bledsoe, Glen.

WITHDRAWN

The world's fastest
helicopters.

Table of Contents

Built for Speed

The World's Fastest Helicopters

by Glen and Karen Bledsoe

Consultant:
U.S. Army
Special Operations Command

CAPSTONE
HIGH-INTEREST
BOOKS

an imprint of Capstone Press
Mankato, Minnesota

Capstone High-Interest Books are published by Capstone Press
151 Good Counsel Drive, P.O. Box 669, Mankato, Minnesota 56002
http://www.capstone-press.com

Library of Congress Cataloging-in-Publication Data
Bledsoe, Glen.
　　The World's fastest helicopters/by Glen and Karen Bledsoe.
　　p. cm.—(Built for speed)
　　Includes bibliographical references and index.
　　Summary: Discusses the history and development of some of the world's fastest
helicopters, describing the specific features and specifications of such aircraft as
the SA 360 Dauphin, Boeing-Sikorsky RAH-66 Comanche, AH-64 Apache, and
V-22 Osprey.
　　ISBN 0-7368-1059-5
　　1. Helicopters—Juvenile literature. 2. Military helicopters—Juvenile literature.
[1. Helicopters. 2. Military helicopters.] I. Bledsoe, Karen E. II. Title. III. Built for
speed (Mankato, Minn.)
TL716.2 .B58 2002
629.133'352—dc21   2001003440

Editorial Credits

Leah K. Pockrandt, editor; Karen Risch, product planning editor; Timothy Halldin,
　　cover designer and illustrator; Katy Kudela, photo researcher

Photo Credits

Boeing Management Company, cover, 24, 27, 31, 39 (top)
Defense Visual Information Center, 28, 37
Digital Vision Ltd., 40
Fotodynamics/Ted Carlson, 18, 21, 32, 39 (bottom)
Hulton Getty/Archive Photos, 7
Intora-Firebird of the United Kingdom, 43
The Military Picture Library/Corbis, 11
Photri-Microstock, 8, 16; Photri-Microstock/B. Howe, 12, 38 (top);
　　Photri-Microstock/Glen Jackson, 15
Richard Zellner/Sikorsky Aircraft Corp., 22, 38 (bottom)
William B. Folsom, 4, 35

1 2 3 4 5 6 07 06 05 04 03 02

Chapter 1

Fast Helicopters

People have been interested in flying for centuries. In 1488, an artist and inventor named Leonardo da Vinci drew a picture of a flying machine. It looked much like a helicopter. Da Vinci's idea may have come from a popular toy called a whirligig.

Da Vinci's drawing was a plan for a rotorcraft. An overhead propeller lifts these flying machines into the air. Da Vinci never built his aircraft. In the 1400s, engines did not exist to power flying machines.

History

In the early 1900s, Henry Berliner created a helicopter. It flew only about 15 feet

Today, Henry Berliner's helicopter is in the College Park Aviation Museum in College Park, Maryland.

(4.6 meters) above the ground for a distance of 100 yards (91 meters). Others also tried to build helicopters. But none of them flew long enough to be practical. No one was successful until Igor Sikorsky.

In 1919, Sikorsky moved to the United States from Russia. In 1923, he formed an aviation company called Sikorsky Aero Engineering Corporation. In 1939, Sikorsky built the VS-300. This aircraft could fly vertically, sideways, and backward. But it could not fly forward. Sikorsky changed the design. On May 6, 1941, he flew the VS-300 for 1 hour, 32 minutes, and 26 seconds.

The VS-300 was the first practical helicopter. It could move in any direction. Today, several types of rotorcraft exist. These aircraft include helicopters, autogyros, and tiltrotors.

Helicopters

A helicopter has one or more motorized overhead rotors. A rotor has two to five blades that spin. The blades allow the pilot to operate the helicopter.

Igor Sikorsky built the first practical helicopter.

Many helicopters have only one large horizontal rotor. This rotor lifts the craft. But it also causes the helicopter to spin in the opposite direction of the blades. Some helicopters have a small vertical tail rotor that faces sideways. This rotor keeps the helicopter from spinning with the force of the overhead rotor. Pilots also use the tail rotor to turn the helicopter.

Some helicopters have two large overhead blades that turn in opposite directions. This

Most helicopters have hinged rotor blades.

movement stops the aircraft from spinning. The blades are either located on top of each other or side by side. Some helicopters also have a blade on the front end and another on the rear.

The rotor blades of most helicopters are hinged. This features allows the blades to tip. The helicopter moves in the direction of the tip.

Autogyros and Tiltrotors

An autogyro looks much like a helicopter. But the two machines work differently. The autogyro has a horizontal overhead blade like a helicopter. But an engine does not rotate the autogyro's blade. A vertical propeller located at the front of the craft pushes the autogyro forward. Air rushes past the horizontal overhead rotor and lifts the autogyro into the air.

Autogyros cannot hover in one spot as helicopters do. But they can make short takeoffs and landings like helicopters.

Tiltrotor aircraft look similar to airplanes. But the wings have propellers attached to them. The rotors tilt horizontally during takeoff like a helicopter's rotors do. The rotors tilt down into a vertical position once the helicopter is in the air. This position pulls the aircraft forward.

Uses of Rotorcraft

Rotorcraft have many advantages over airplanes. They can turn quickly and fly in any direction. They can fly close to the ground. Some can hover. Rotorcraft need little space in which to land and take off. Rotorcraft can fly in strong winds. Rotors have the same ability to lift despite the direction of the wind.

Rotorcraft have many uses. Some people fly small rotorcraft for sport. Some companies offer sight-seeing helicopter rides. People often use helicopters to search for or rescue missing or injured people. Rescuers also use rotorcraft to carry cargo to remote locations and to fight fires.

The U.S. military uses the world's fastest helicopters. The military uses many of these helicopters to rescue wounded soldiers. It uses specially equipped helicopters to spy on enemies. The military also uses some helicopters in combat.

This Westland Lynx is similar to the Lynx that was used to break the speed record.

A specially-designed helicopter set the world speed record in 1986. This helicopter is a Lynx. A British company called Westland makes the Lynx. The record-setting Lynx had high-speed, lightweight rotor blades.

On August 11, 1986, a Lynx reached a speed of 249.09 miles (400.87 kilometers) per hour. It set the record on a 9.3-mile (15-kilometer) course.

The Lynx is an anti-tank helicopter. It is equipped with weapons powerful enough to destroy a tank. The Lynx is powered by two Rolls-Royce Gem 41 engines. The maximum speed of a standard Lynx helicopter is 205 miles (330 kilometers) per hour. A helicopter's range is the distance it can travel without refueling. The Lynx's range is 53 miles (85 kilometers).

Chapter 2

Dauphin and Panther

A company in France called Eurocopter makes several types of helicopters. These include two similar light- to medium-weight helicopters. The SA 360 Dauphin is for civilian use. The AS 565 Panther is for military use.

SA 360 Dauphin

The SA 360 Dauphin is a single-engine helicopter. It was first flown in 1972.

Combat helicopters have landing gear that retracts. The pilot can pull the landing gear safely inside the helicopter. But pilots do not use the Dauphin in combat. It does not need to protect its landing gear. The Dauphin's landing gear is fixed.

The Dauphin's landing gear does not retract.

People use the Dauphin to travel to hard-to-reach places. Pilots can land the Dauphin on boats, rooftops, and other small areas.

Hospitals and rescue services use the Dauphin to carry injured or sick people to hospitals. Some hospital landing pads are on the hospitals' roofs.

Many police and fire departments also use the Dauphin. They use the helicopter to search for lost or injured people. They also use it to transport fire fighters and police officers to areas where they are needed.

The Dauphin is useful as a rescue helicopter because of its speed. The Dauphin can reach a speed of 196 miles (315 kilometers) per hour.

The AS 565 Panther

The AS 565 Panther is the military version of the Dauphin. It first flew in 1973. The tails of the AS 565 and the SA 360 Dauphin are similar. The helicopters are very different in most other ways.

The Panther is used to bring soldiers and cargo to battle sites. The Panther's landing gear retracts to protect it from enemy weapons. The

Many police departments use the Dauphin for search-and-rescue work.

Panther also is used to bring wounded soldiers to hospitals.

The Panther can carry a great deal of weight. Two pilots fly each helicopter. The Panther can carry eight to 10 soldiers. It also can carry weapons, medicine, and supplies.

The AS 565 SB is a Panther that is armed with weapons. The AS 565 SB can be carried

aboard combat ships at sea. Pilots may use it to gather information about an enemy's position. The AS 565 SB also can launch attacks from a ship. It can carry cannons and missiles to destroy aircraft and tanks. It also can carry rockets and torpedoes. These weapons are used to destroy ships and submarines.

The AS 565 SB flies slower than the Dauphin. The weapons add extra weight to the helicopter. The AS 565 SB can reach speeds of 184 miles (296 kilometers) per hour.

The AS 565 and AS 565 SB both have a four-blade rotor on top of the aircraft. The rotor is turned by two turboshaft engines. Each engine produces 749 horsepower. This unit measures the engine's power. The helicopter's range is 506 miles (814 kilometers).

The Panther is used as a military transport and combat helicopter.

Chapter 3

RAH-66 Comanche

The RAH-66 Comanche is a new type of helicopter. Boeing and Sikorsky Aircraft Corporation build this small, fast helicopter. It can reach speeds of 204 miles (328 kilometers) per hour.

The U.S. Army plans to begin using this helicopter in 2006. The Comanche will replace older attack and observation helicopters.

The Comanche's Mission

The Comanche does not carry supplies or troops. It is a reconnaissance helicopter. The U.S. military uses these helicopters to scout out areas and search for enemy soldiers. This information is sent back to support troops. The military has used other helicopters for

The U.S. Army plans to begin using the RAH-66 Comanche in 2006.

reconnaissance. But the Comanche is the first helicopter designed for that purpose only.

The Comanche is equipped with special visual and electronic sensors. These devices help crew members identify and locate enemy weapon systems. The sensors allow the helicopter to operate at night and in bad weather.

The Comanche's Engine

The Comanche has twin turboshaft engines. A turboshaft engine creates hot air to turn the helicopter's five-blade rotor. Each engine produces 1,300 horsepower.

The Comanche's engines are different than other helicopter engines. The engines have a high thrust-to-weight ratio. They produce a great deal of power compared to their weight. Thrust is the force that moves helicopters forward. Thrust is measured in pounds.

Weapons

The Comanche will be armed with weapons. Crew members can attack targets on the ground or direct support troops to enemy targets. The Comanche also can serve as a combat aircraft against other aircraft in the air. Special equipment

The Comanche's twin turboshaft engines each produce 1,300 horsepower.

helps the gunner quickly target an enemy. The gunner targets and fires the Comanche's weapons. The Comanche will be teamed with the AH-64D Apache Longbow. These two attack helicopters can trade electronic information easily.

The Comanche carries a three-barrel General Electric Gatling gun mounted on a turret. This device turns to allow crew members to fire the gun in many directions. A motor powers the turret. Electronic sensors will not allow the gun to fire at targets that are too far away to hit.

The Comanche is loaded with different types of weapons.

The Comanche can carry different types of missiles and rockets. The missiles are mounted on the weapon bay doors. The doors open sideways from the aircraft.

Pilots will wear a special kind of helmet during missions. The helmet is connected to the helicopter's computer system. The helmet visor contains an electronic display screen. The display screen shows information about enemy targets. Sensors inside the helmet tell the computer when the pilot's head turns. The computer can lock onto the targets that the pilot looks at. The helmets will allow pilots to fire weapons very quickly.

The Comanche's Design

The Comanche is hard for enemy soldiers to see, hear, or detect with radar. Radar uses radio waves to find distant aircraft and objects. Machines and people give off heat. Heat rays are called infrared rays. Weapon instruments can detect infrared. The Comanche has shields to hide its infrared rays.

The Comanche will need little maintenance. Pilots can easily replace many of the helicopter parts. This ability is an advantage when pilots are on long-distance missions. The Comanche also uses less fuel than other helicopters. This feature gives the Comanche a longer range than other helicopters. The Comanche has a range of 1,406 miles (2,263 kilometers). To reach this range, the helicopter must be equipped with extra gas tanks.

Chapter 4

AH-64 Apache

The AH-64 Apache is the world's fastest attack helicopter. It can attack enemies on the ground or in the air. The Apache can fly missions during the day and night. It also can fly in all types of weather.

The McDonnell Douglas Aircraft Company started building Apaches in the mid-1980s. This company is now part of Boeing McDonnell Douglas Helicopter Systems. The U.S. Army began using Apaches in 1984.

In 1997, Boeing began making a more advanced helicopter model called the AH-64D Apache Longbow. The U.S. military uses both the Apache AH-64A and Longbow.

The Apache's speed makes it the world's fastest attack helicopter.

AH-64A Apache Features

The Apache looks different than most other helicopters. It has a narrow body. The sides are shaped like a block. Short wings attach to its sides. The wings carry racks of rockets and missiles.

Each Apache carries a pilot and a co-pilot gunner (CPG). Apache pilots and CPGs wear a special kind of helmet during missions. The helmet is similar to the helmets worn by Comanche pilots.

The Apache Engines

Two General Electric T700 turboshaft engines power the Apache AH-64A. Turboshaft engines create hot air to turn helicopters' rotors. Each of the Apache's engines produces almost 1,700 horsepower.

The Apache has two rotors. The main rotor has four blades. It is located behind the cockpit. The Apache also has a tail rotor.

The Apache's maximum speed is 232 miles (374 kilometers) per hour. The Apache's range is 1,180 miles (1,899 kilometers) without extra fuel tanks.

The Apache's body is narrower than other helicopters.

AH-64A Apache Weapons

The Apache AH-64A carries many types of weapons. It has a machine gun turret under its nose. This turret is linked to infrared sensors and special cameras that help the CPG find targets.

The Apache carries an M230 machine gun. This gun is mounted under the helicopter.

The Apache's most important weapon is the AGM-114 Hellfire missile. The Hellfire is a

The Apache's weapons include Hydra rockets.

laser-guided missile. The Apache's CPG points
a laser beam at a target on the ground. The
crew member then fires the missile. The
Hellfire includes sensors that detect the laser
beam. The missile then strikes the beam's
target. The Hellfire often is fired at tanks. The
missile includes a powerful explosive that can
destroy tough tank armor.

Apaches also carry Hydra rockets. These powerful explosives fly like missiles. But Hydra rockets are not guided. They fly in a straight line. They carry many small explosives called bomblets.

Apache helicopters are the first combat helicopters able to fly in darkness. The Apache has a sensor to help the pilot fly in the dark. These helicopters also use laser and infrared systems to find enemy targets.

The Apache is a well-armored aircraft. It can withstand direct hits from large ammunition without major damage.

The Apache AH-64D Longbow

The Apache AH-64D Longbow is the newest Apache helicopter. It has many of the same weapons and sensors as the Apache AH-64A. It also has many new features that make it more well-equipped than the AH-64A.

The Apache Longbow is the only helicopter in service that has a digitized acquisition system. This computerized system is able to detect enemy targets. The system identifies the target. The pilot then can decide whether to fire at the target. The identification process takes less than 30 seconds.

The Longbow can share the information it gathers. It can send electronic information to other aircraft and to troops on the ground. This ability gives the Longbow a strong advantage over other combat helicopters. The digital system makes the Longbow even deadlier than the AH-64A.

Longbow Weapons

The Longbow is more heavily armored than the AH-64A. The Longbow can survive with more damage than the Apache. The Longbow's heavy armor provides greater protection for the pilot and crew.

The Longbow carries both new and updated weapons. These weapons include a new type of Hellfire missile. A laser does not guide this new missile. Instead, the missile has a small

The Apache Longbow has heavy armor for greater protection against enemy fire.

radar device in its nose. The radar guides the missile to its target. This feature allows Apache CPGs to fire more than one missile at once.

Its advanced features make the Longbow the fastest and deadliest combat helicopter in the world. In time, it will replace the AH-64A.

Chapter 5

V-22 Osprey

The world's fastest type of rotorcraft also is one of the most unusual. Bell Helicopter Textron, Inc. and Boeing make the Osprey. The Bell-Boeing V-22 Osprey series rotorcrafts are tiltrotor aircraft. Like other helicopters, the rotors are used for vertical takeoff. But the rotors also can be tilted forward. The aircraft then can fly like an airplane.

The Osprey's tilted rotors allow it to fly much faster than most helicopters. Its top speed is 316 miles (509 kilometers) per hour with its airplane function. That speed is about twice as fast as most high-speed helicopters. In helicopter function, the V-22 Osprey can travel at about 115 miles (185 kilometers) per hour.

The Osprey has an unusual design.

The tiltrotor design has many advantages besides speed. The Osprey has a range of more than 2,335 miles (3,758 kilometers). This distance is about twice as far as other long-range helicopters can fly. A long-range rotorcraft can launch from ships farther from shore. Enemies then cannot plan defense strategies as easily.

The tiltrotor design allows the Osprey to take off and land vertically like other helicopters. But it can fly as fast and far as a propeller-driven airplane. These features make tiltrotor aircraft ideal for rescue situations. The U.S. Navy and Marine Corps hope to use the Osprey craft for rescue operations.

Osprey Models

Bell-Boeing builds two Osprey models. The U.S. Marine Corps uses both the MV-22 and the CV-22. But the U.S. Air Force only uses the CV-22. The MV-22 Osprey is designed to carry troops into an area after a first attack. It also can carry supplies and equipment or rescue troops from dangerous areas.

The long-range Osprey can launch from ships that are far from shore.

The Osprey is designed to perform special missions. One such task is the rescue of downed airplane pilots in enemy territory. The MV-22 can carry 24 armed soldiers. It can lift loads as heavy as 10,000 pounds (4,536 kilograms). The Osprey is designed to operate in any kind of weather during the day or at night.

The CV-22 is a special version of the Osprey. It is designed for the harshest and most dangerous conditions. It was built to fly into enemy territory at low levels.

Dangerous Design

The U.S. military makes limited use of the Osprey because of the craft's poor safety record. In 1999, two Osprey crashes killed 23 Marines. The U.S. military stopped using all Osprey aircraft after the second crash.

One possible cause of the crashes is damage to the Osprey's hydraulic systems. The Osprey has three hydraulic systems that move the engines and adjust the rotors. The systems are powered by fluid forced through pipelike chambers. Some investigators believe that the system was faulty and interfered with control of the craft. Investigators also looked at the maintenance records. They discovered that the Ospreys had been properly maintained.

Human error can cause tiltrotor aircraft to crash. The Osprey operates both as a helicopter and a propeller-driven airplane. Pilots need special training and a great deal of practice to

Osprey pilots need to be able to fly both helicopters and airplanes.

fly the craft. Few pilots are equally skilled in flying both helicopters and airplanes.

The entire Osprey V-22 program is under review. The U.S. government is concerned about the crashes. Some Marine Corps officers were accused of covering up the safety records. The government also is concerned about the cost of the aircraft. The Osprey is very expensive. Each aircraft costs $40.1 million.

FAST FACTS

THE SA 360 DAUPHIN

Built By:	Eurocopter
Engines:	One turboshaft
Length:	36 feet (10.9 meters)
Height:	11.6 feet (3.5 meters)
Weight:	3,439 pounds
(empty)	(1,560 kilograms)
Range:	408 miles
	(657 kilometers)
Top Speed:	196 miles
	(315 kilometers)
	per hour

THE RAH-66 COMANCHE

Built By:	Boeing and Sikorsky Aircraft Corporation
Engines:	Two turboshafts
Length:	43.4 feet (13.2 meters)
Height:	11.1 feet (3.4 meters)
Weight:	7,749 pounds
(empty)	(3,515 kilograms)
Range:	1,406 miles
	(2,263 kilometers)
Top Speed:	204 miles
	(328 kilometers)
	per hour

THE AH-64 APACHE

Built By:	Boeing McDonnell Douglas Helicopter Systems
Engines:	Two T700-GE-701Cs
Length:	58 feet (17.7 meters)
Height:	15.3 feet (4.6 meters)
Weight: (empty)	11,800 pounds (5,352 kilograms)
Range:	1,180 miles (1,899 kilometers)
Top Speed:	232 miles (374 kilometers) per hour

THE MV-22 OSPREY

Built By:	Bell Helicopter Textron, Inc. and Boeing
Engines:	Two turboshafts
Length:	57.4 feet (17.5 meters)
Height:	17.8 feet (5.4 meters)
Weight: (empty)	31,886 pounds (14,463 kilograms)
Range:	2,335 miles (3,758 kilometers)
Top Airplane Speed:	316 miles (509 kilometers) per hour
Top Helicopter Speed:	115 miles (185 kilometers) per hour

Chapter 6

Future of Fast Helicopters

Helicopters will continue to get faster as engineers create new designs. These engineers are working on new types of rotorcraft and safer tiltrotor models than the Osprey. Engineers also are working on new and cleaner fuels for all helicopters.

Safe tiltrotor aircraft could have many uses. Both civilians and military members could use it for rescue missions and to carry injured people. Tiltrotor aircraft also would be useful after natural disasters such as fires, floods, hurricanes, and earthquakes.

Tiltrotor craft could be used for passenger service. Tiltrotor aircraft can be built to carry as many people as small shuttle jets can.

Companies will continue to improve the safety and quality of helicopters and the fuels that they use.

Future Fuel

In 1997, a British company called Intora-Firebird purchased the design for a one-person helicopter that has no engine. In 1998, the company introduced the aircraft. The helicopter uses a chemical called hydrogen peroxide as its fuel. Diluted hydrogen peroxide is sold in stores. It is used to disinfect or clean cuts. Only special suppliers sell concentrated hydrogen peroxide. This chemical can explode if used improperly.

The Firebird carries a tank of concentrated hydrogen peroxide. It has tiny rocket motors at the tips of its rotor blades. Hydrogen peroxide is forced through tubes into the motors.

In the motors, the hydrogen peroxide has a chemical reaction with a mesh that is made from stainless steel and silver. This action causes the hydrogen peroxide to break down into steam and oxygen. The process is rapid and explosive. The motors then release the steam and oxygen at a rapid rate. This action causes the rotors to turn. It creates no pollution.

The Firebird is fast for a one-person helicopter. It has achieved speeds as fast as 100 miles (161 kilometers) per hour.

The Firebird is a one-person helicopter.

Some people believe that these helicopters would be useful as personal aircraft. People could use the Firebird in addition to automobiles. But British aviation officials are worried about how to regulate small personal aircraft.

Intora-Firebird also is trying to interest the British military in its helicopter. The Firebird can take off and land more easily than standard helicopters.

Words to Know

ammunition (am-yuh-NISH-uhn)—objects that can be shot from a weapon; bullets and bombs are types of ammunition.

hydraulic system (hye-DRAW-lik SISS-tuhm)—a system powered by fluid forced through pipelike chambers

propeller (pruh-PEL-ur)—a set of rotating blades that provides the force to move an aircraft through the air

radar (RAY-dar)—equipment that uses radio waves to locate and guide objects

reconnaissance (ree-CAH-nuh-suhns)—a mission to gather information about an enemy

rotor (ROH-tur)—machinery that spins a set of rotating blades; rotors allow helicopter pilots to lift or steer an aircraft.

rotorcraft (ROH-tur-kraft)—an aircraft such as a helicopter that uses a rotor to fly

To Learn More

Genat, Robert. *Choppers: Thunder in the Sky.* New York: MetroBooks, 1998.

Pitt, Matthew. *Apache Helicopter: The AH-64.* High-Tech Military Weapons. New York: Children's Press, 2000.

Schleifer, Jay. *Combat Helicopters.* Wings. Mankato, Minn.: Capstone Books, 1996.

Stille, Darlene R. *Helicopters.* A True Book. New York: Children's Press, 1997.

Sweetman, Bill. *Attack Helicopters: The AH-64 Apaches.* War Planes. Mankato, Minn.: Capstone High-Interest Books, 2001.

Useful Addresses

Helicopter Association of Canada
1421 50 O'Connor Street
Ottawa, ON K1P 6L2
Canada

National Air and Space Museum
Seventh and Independence Avenue SW
Washington, DC 20560

The Popular Rotorcraft Association
  Headquarters
P.O. Box 68
Mentone, IN 46539

Internet Sites

Boeing Rotorcraft
http://www.boeing.com/rotorcraft

The Helicopter History Site
http://www.helis.com

Igor I. Sikorsky Historical Archives Inc.
http://www.sikorskyarchives.com

Naval Aviation Systems TEAM
http://www.navair.navy.mil

Web site for Defence Industries—Army: RAH-66 Comanche Reconnaissance/ Attack Helicopter, USA
http://www.army-technology.com/projects/ comanche/index.html

Index